CROAKERS

ROGER

Cartoons by
Don Dougherty

WARNER BOOKS

A Warner Communications Company

D1529648

Warner Books, Inc., 75 Rockefeller Plaza, New York, N.Y. 10019.

W A Warner Communications Company.

Printed in the United States of America

First printing: September 1982
10 9 8 7 6 5 4 3 2

Library of Congress Cataloging in Publication Data

Dougherty, Don.
Croakers.

1. American wit and humor, Pictorial. I. Title.
NC1429.D58A4   1982   741.5'973   82-8623

ISBN 0-446-37245-5 (U.S.A.)   AACR2
ISBN 0-446-37282-X (Canada)

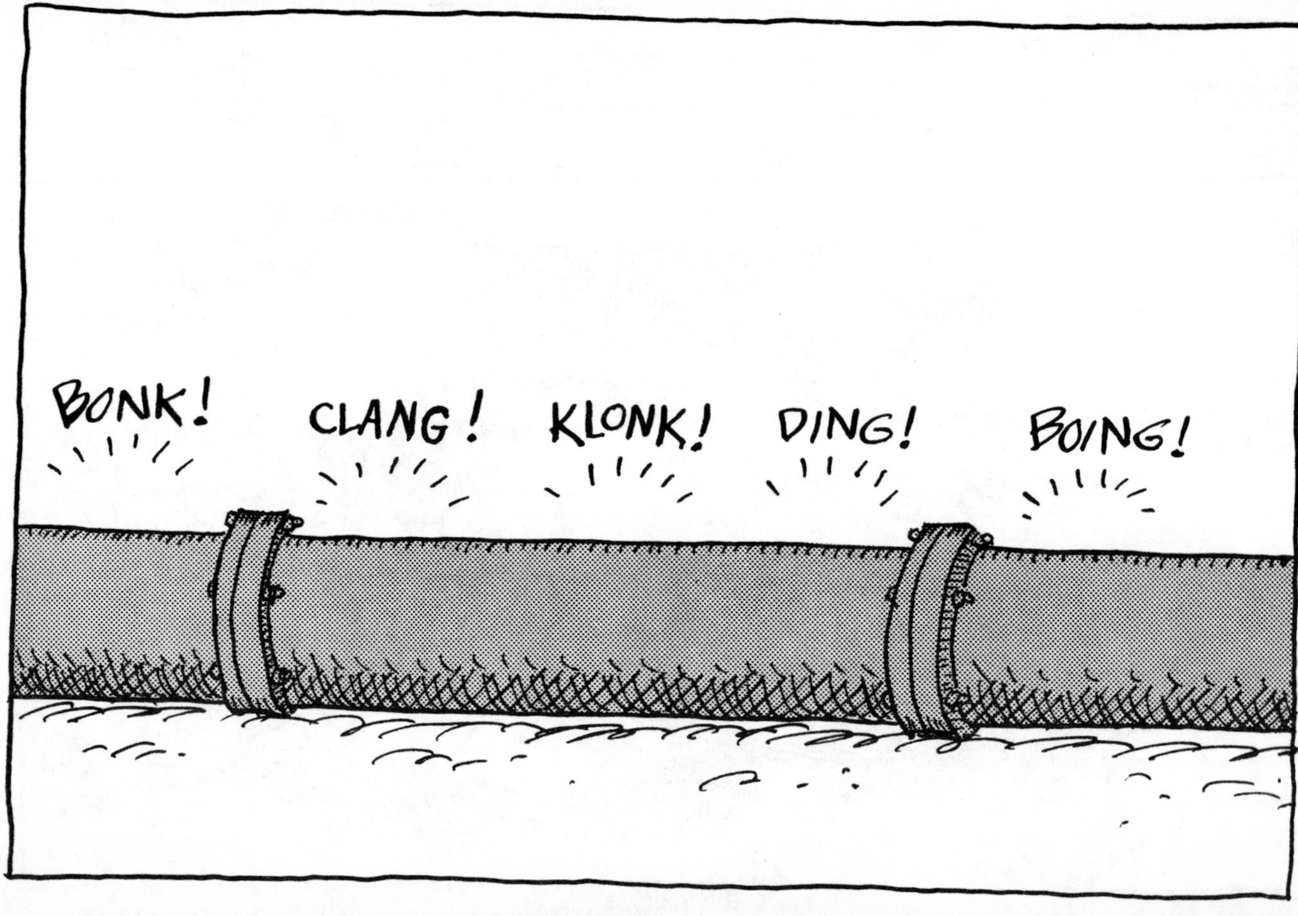
BONK!
CLANG!
KLONK!
DING!
BOING!

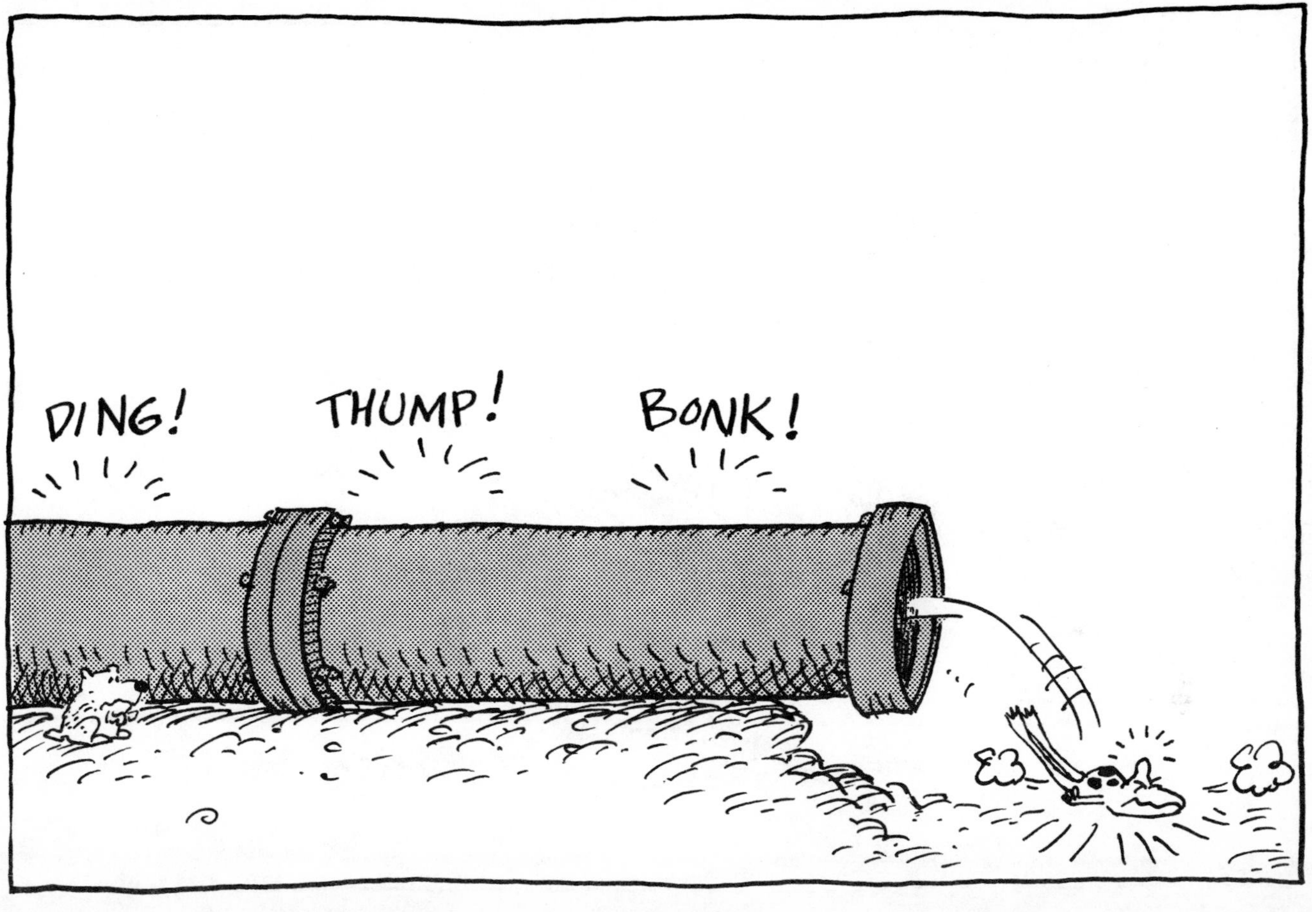
DING!
THUMP!
BONK!

VRRRRRRRRR

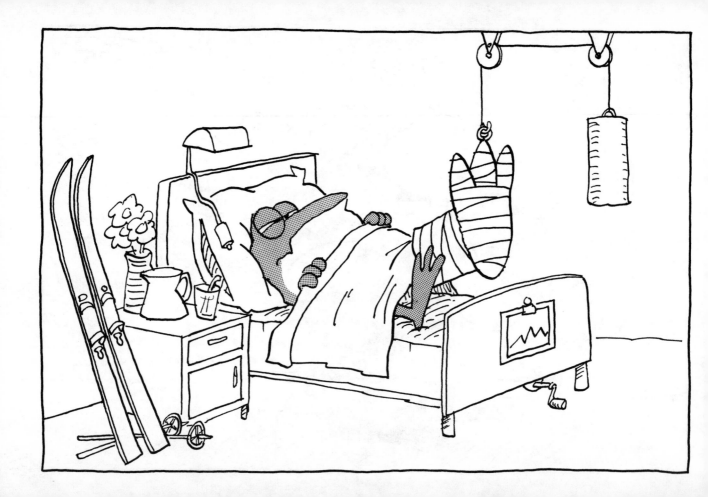

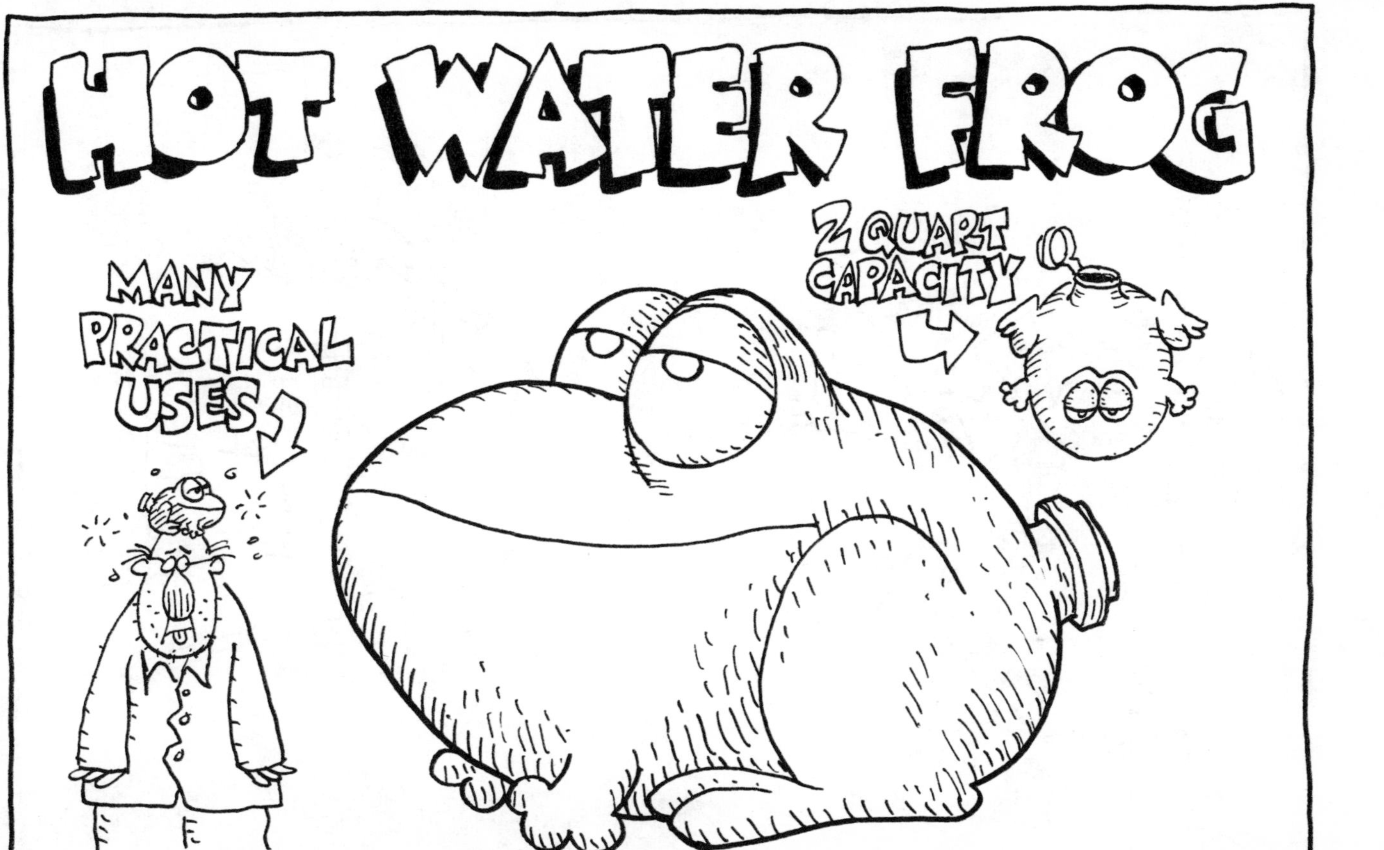
HOT WATER FROG
2 QUART CAPACITY
MANY PRACTICAL USES

CROAKER CLASSICS   "MOBY FLY"

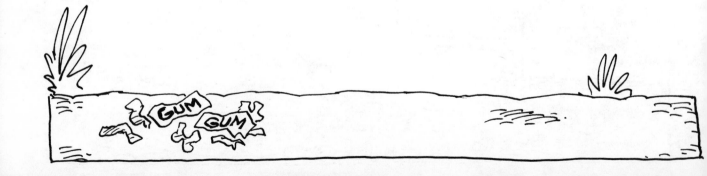

MAKING YOUR VERY OWN CROAKERS HAND PUPPET

GREEN FELT

STRIP OF TAPE

(PUT TAPE ON FINGER)

BUTTON EYES

CARDBOARD FLAPS
(CUT ON DOTTED LINES)

RED FOOD DYE
(PUT ON FINGER)

FOOD DYE

3.